God's ГПЕ UПЕ
Who Thought of It First!

Written by
Joan N. Keener

Illustrated by
Stephen Carpenter

The Standard Publishing Company, Cincinnati, Ohio. A division of Standex International Corporation.
© 1998 by The Standard Publishing Company.
Printed in the United States of America. All rights reserved.
Designed by Coleen Davis. Graphic Layout by Dale Meyers.
Edited by Laura Ring.

Library of Congress Catalog Card Number 97-46806. Cataloging-in-Publication data available.
ISBN 0-7847-0832-0.

Scripture on page 24 from the *International Children's Bible, New Century Version.*
© 1986, 1988 by Word Publishing, Dallas, Texas 75039. Used by permission.

STANDARD
PUBLISHING
Cincinnati, Ohio

People invent all sorts of fun and useful things. They use their imaginations and come up with exciting ideas. Have you ever wondered where those ideas come from?

God made our imaginations. He is the first and the best inventor. So next time you see a terrific invention, remember . . .

God's the one who thought of it first!

A **surfboard** is smooth and has a fin underneath so surfers can ride the waves with speed and turn easily.

But God's the one who thought of it first!

He made the . . .

Dolphin

The dolphin's smooth body and strong back fin help him move quickly and easily through the waves.

People build **dams** made of metal
and concrete to hold back the
flow of water.

But God's the one who thought of it first!

He made the . . .

Beaver

Beavers use logs, branches, and rocks glued together with mud to hold back water so they can build homes on the river.

Night vision goggles use the light from the stars and moon to allow soldiers to see better at night.

But God's the one who thought of it first!

He made the . . .

Cat

Cats can see well at night because
shiny layers at the back of their
eyes reflect light.

You can use a straw to drink from a glass.

But God's the one who thought of it first!

He made the . . .

LEMONADE
5¢

Butterfly

The butterfly's mouth forms a long sucking tube for drinking nectar from flowers.

When you swim underwater, flippers can
help your feet push the water so you
can move forward.

But God's the one who thought of it first!

He made the . . .

Duck

The duck's webbed feet push the water back so she can swim.

You use a **flashlight** to help you see other people and things in the dark.

But God's the one who thought of it first!

He made the . . .

Firefly

Chemicals in this insect's body flash light to signal other fireflies and find them in the dark.

Construction workers use a **jackhammer** to drill into rock or pavement.

But God's the one who thought of it first!

He made the . . .

Woodpecker

The woodpecker has a long,
hard bill for drilling into trees.

Scuba divers wear **wet suits** so they can swim faster and stay warm in cold water.

But God's the one who thought of it first!

He made the . . .

Seal

Their smooth coats and thick layers of blubber help seals swim quickly and stay warm in the cold water.

Photographers on safari wear camouflage so the animals won't see them and run away.

But God's the one who thought of it first!

He made the . . .

Chameleon

The chameleon's skin changes colors to match
the surroundings so his enemies won't see him.

Radar waves bounce off objects like an echo.
Pilots of ships and planes use radar at night to
measure distances and find objects
in their paths.

But God's the one who thought of it first!

He made the . . .

Bat

This animal makes a high-pitched cry that bounces off objects and comes back to the bat's ears like an echo. Bats use their radar at night to measure distances and identify objects.

You can see God's imagination working everywhere in our world. We have wonderful ideas, but

God's the one who thought of them first!

"Ask the animals,
and they will teach you.
Or ask the birds of the air,
and they will tell you.
Speak to the earth,
and it will teach you.
Or let the fish of the sea tell you.
Every one of these knows
that the hand of the Lord
has done this."
Job 12:7-9

For many years, Joan Keener has collected examples like the ones in this book. She would like to hear from readers who have examples to share with her. Write to Joan Keener in care of Standard Publishing, Children's Books, 8121 Hamilton Avenue, Cincinnati, OH 45231.